LIFE IS...

Created, published, and distributed by Knock Knock
1635 Electric Ave.
Venice, CA 90291
knockknockstuff.com
Knock Knock is a registered trademark of Knock Knock LLC

© 2018 Knock Knock LLC
All rights reserved
Printed in China

Design by Carol Kono-Noble
Illustrations by Harriet Russell

No part of this product may be used or reproduced in any manner whatsoever without prior written permission from the publisher, except in the case of brief quotations embodied in critical articles and reviews. For information, address Knock Knock.

Where specific company, product, and brand names are cited, copyright and trademarks associated with these names are property of their respective owners. Every reasonable attempt has been made to identify owners of copyright. Errors or omissions will be corrected in subsequent editions.

ISBN: 978-168349083-8
UPC: 825703-50215-2

10 9 8 7 6 5 4 3 2 1

LIFE IS...
SWEET
(and other such sayings)

KNOCK KNOCK.
VENICE, CALIFORNIA

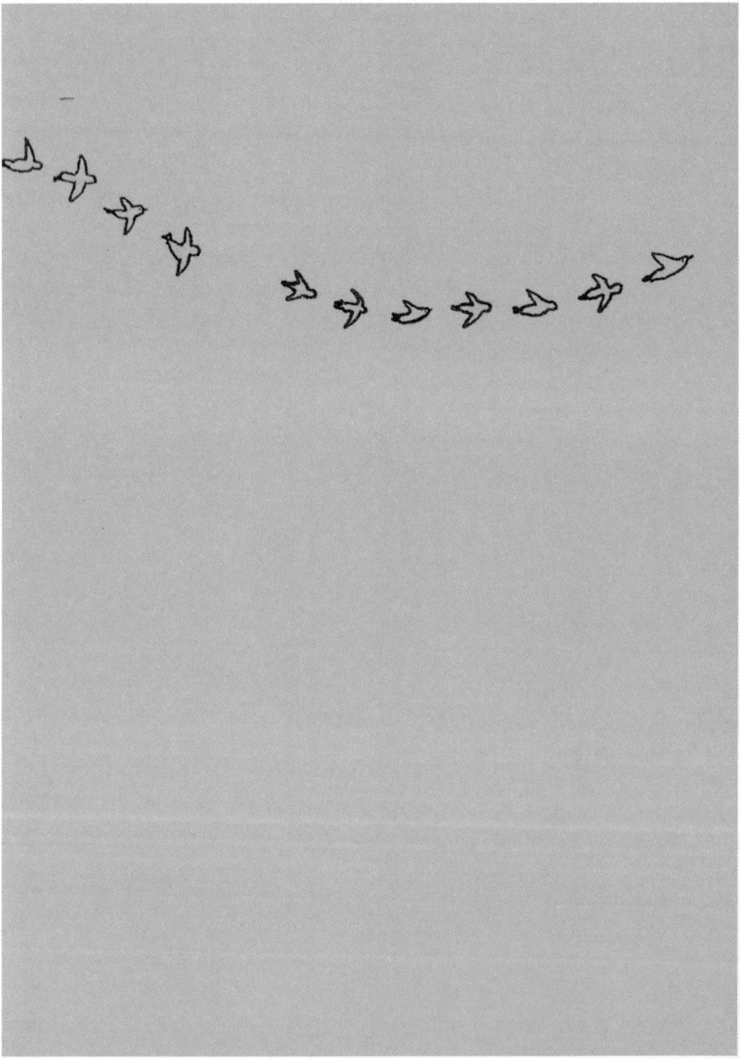

DESCRIBING
THE INTANGIBLE

It's pretty obvious that the biggest philosophical questions are notoriously hard to answer. That's why humans turn to comparisons to explain the mysteries of the universe. It's easier to describe one mysterious and incomprehensible thing by noting its similarities to other, more familiar and concrete things.

Ask someone to finish the phrase "Life is…" and you might hear a proverb, a quotation, a saying, or a song lyric. Often, you'll hear a metaphor of some kind. There are as many ways to describe what "life is" as there are grains of sand on a beach (there's another metaphor—we just can't help ourselves).

But they don't all have the same perspective. Great minds may think alike, but you'll see as you page through this book that there are as many points of view about the subject of "life" as there are stars in the sky (see how easy that is?). Watch how the examples, both cynical and sweet, within this little book complement—and contradict—each other.

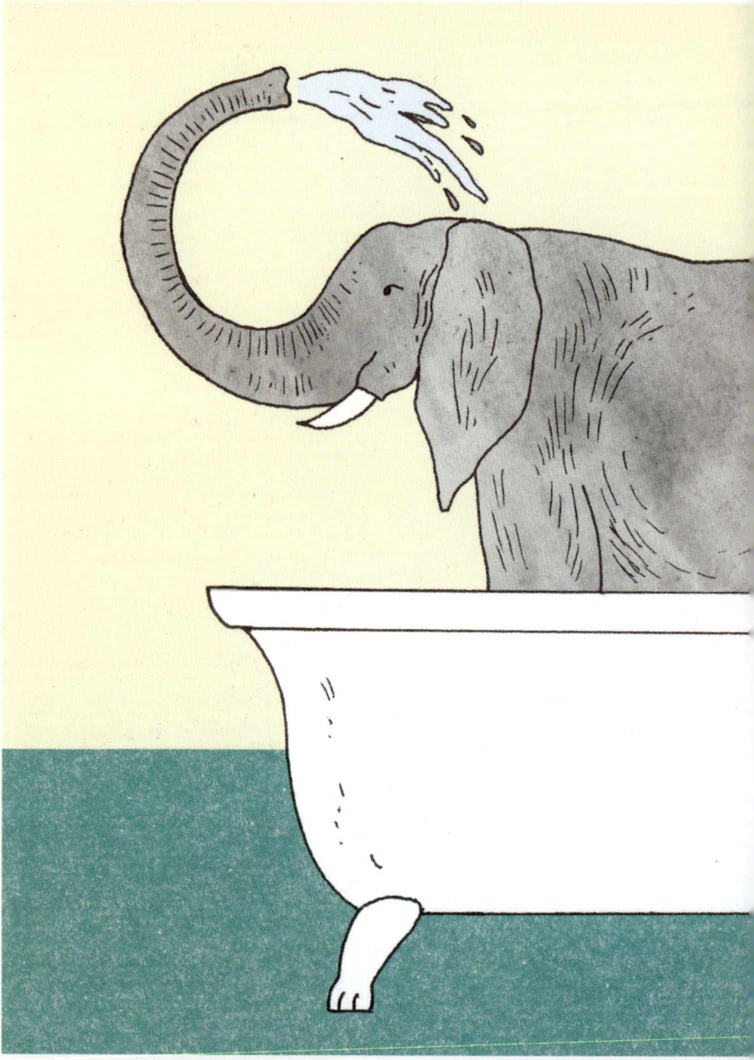

Life is like a bath:
the longer you're in
the more wrinkled
you get.

Life is crazy.

Life is messy.

LIFE IS A ONE-TIME OFFER.

Life is
a succession
of moments.

Life is a roller coaster.

LIFE IS LIKE AN ELEVATOR: IT HAS ITS UPS AND DOWNS.

LIFE IS
WHAT
HAPPENS
TO YOU
WHILE
YOU'RE
BUSY
MAKING
OTHER
PLANS.

LIFE IS A GAME.

LIFE IS NOT A COMPETITION.

LIFE IS LIKE A GRINDSTONE: WHETHER IT GRINDS YOU DOWN OR POLISHES YOU UP DEPENDS ON WHAT YOU ARE MADE OF.

LIFE IS A BEAUTIFUL STRUGGLE.

LIFE IS JUST ONE DAMN THING AFTER ANOTHER.

Life is a series of choices.

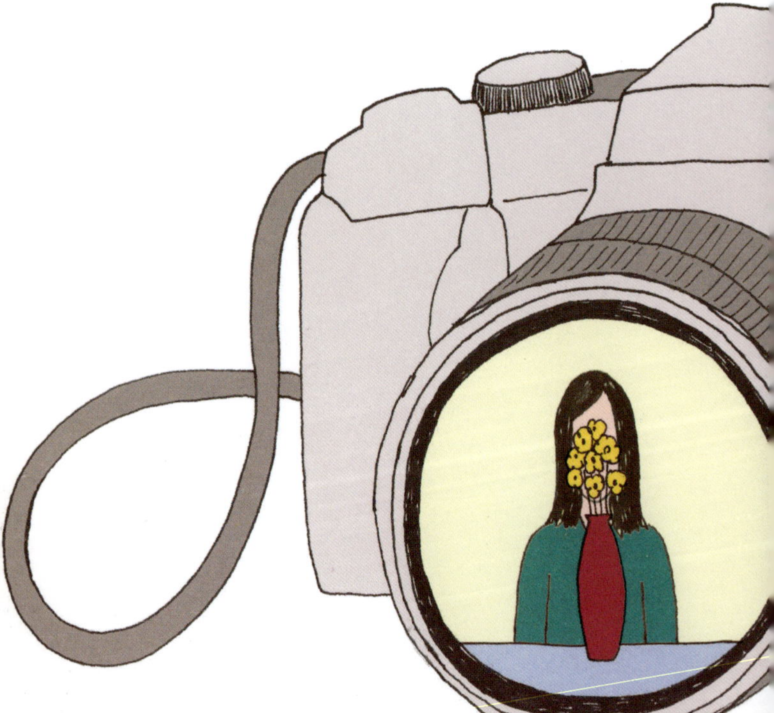

Life is like a camera: just focus on what's important, capture the good times, develop from the negatives, and if things don't work out, take another shot.

LIFE IS A ZEN KOAN.

LIFE IS A STORY.

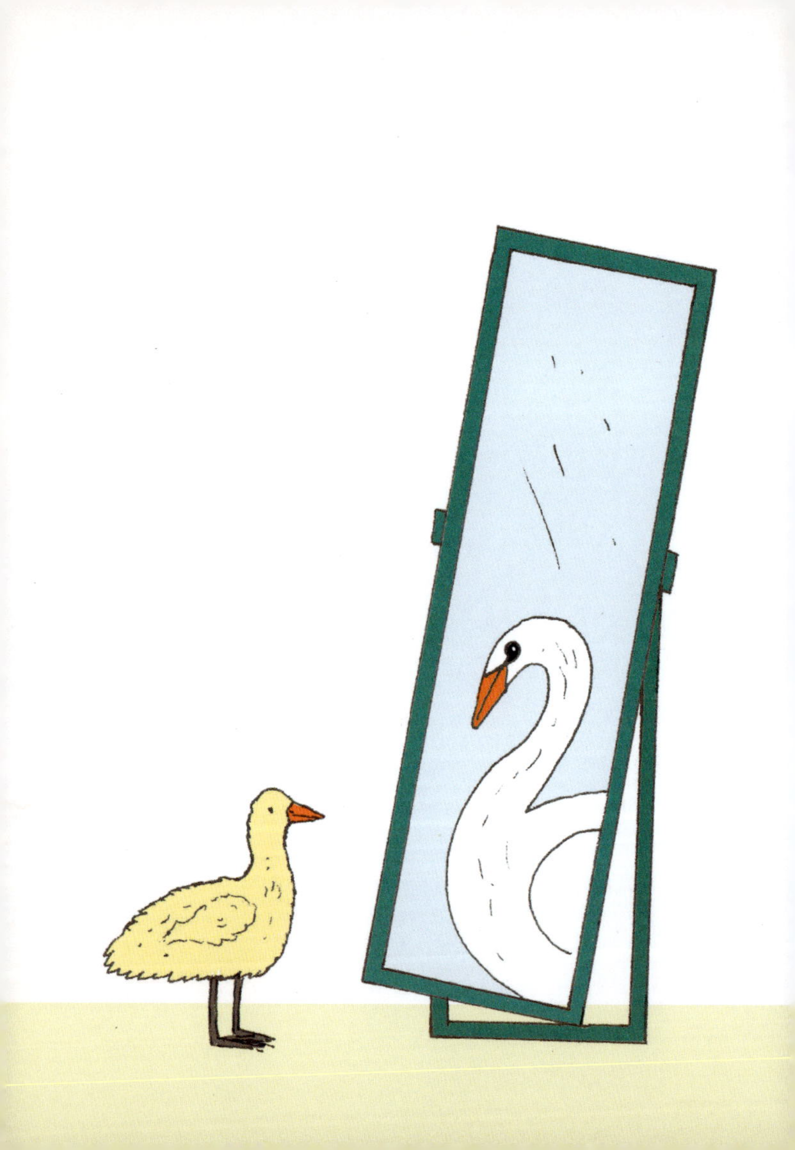

LIFE IS
A MIRROR.

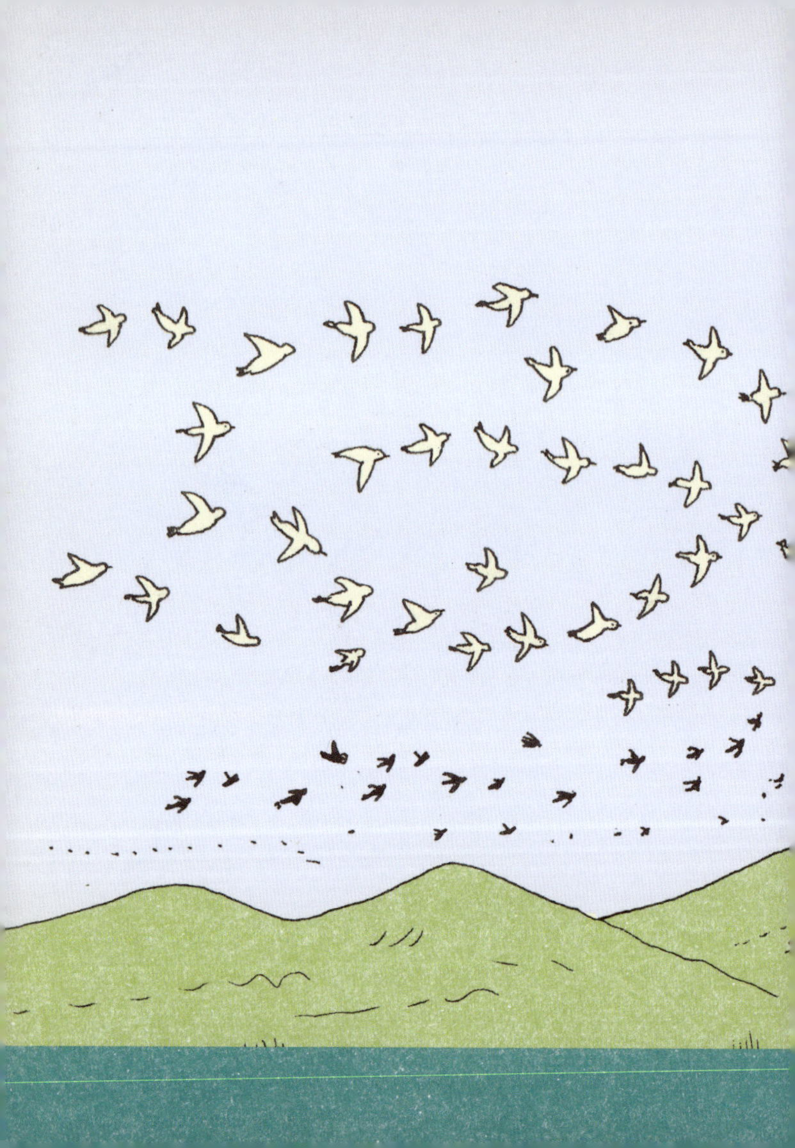

LIFE IS A JOURNEY.

Life is long.

Life is short.

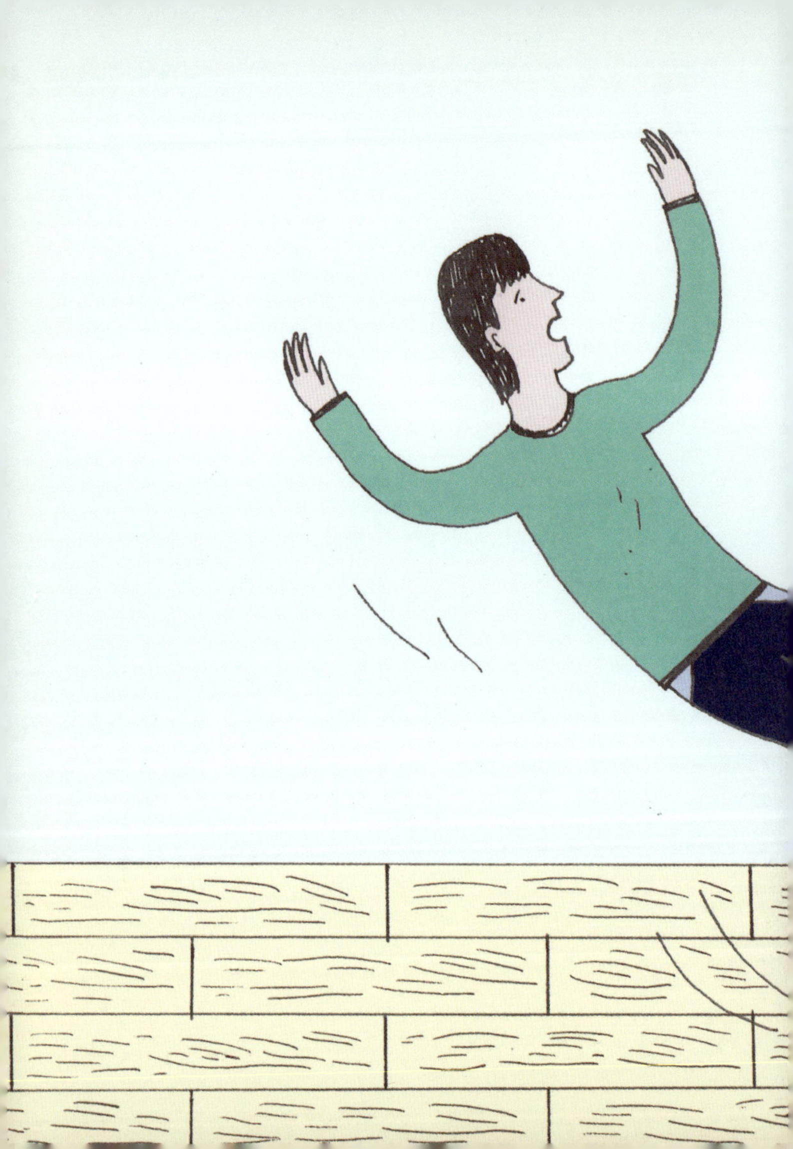

LIFE IS NOT HAVING BEEN TOLD THAT THE MAN HAS JUST WAXED THE FLOOR.

Life is hard.

LIFE IS
WHAT
YOU
MAKE
OF IT.

LIFE IS REAL.

LIFE IS BUT A DREAM.

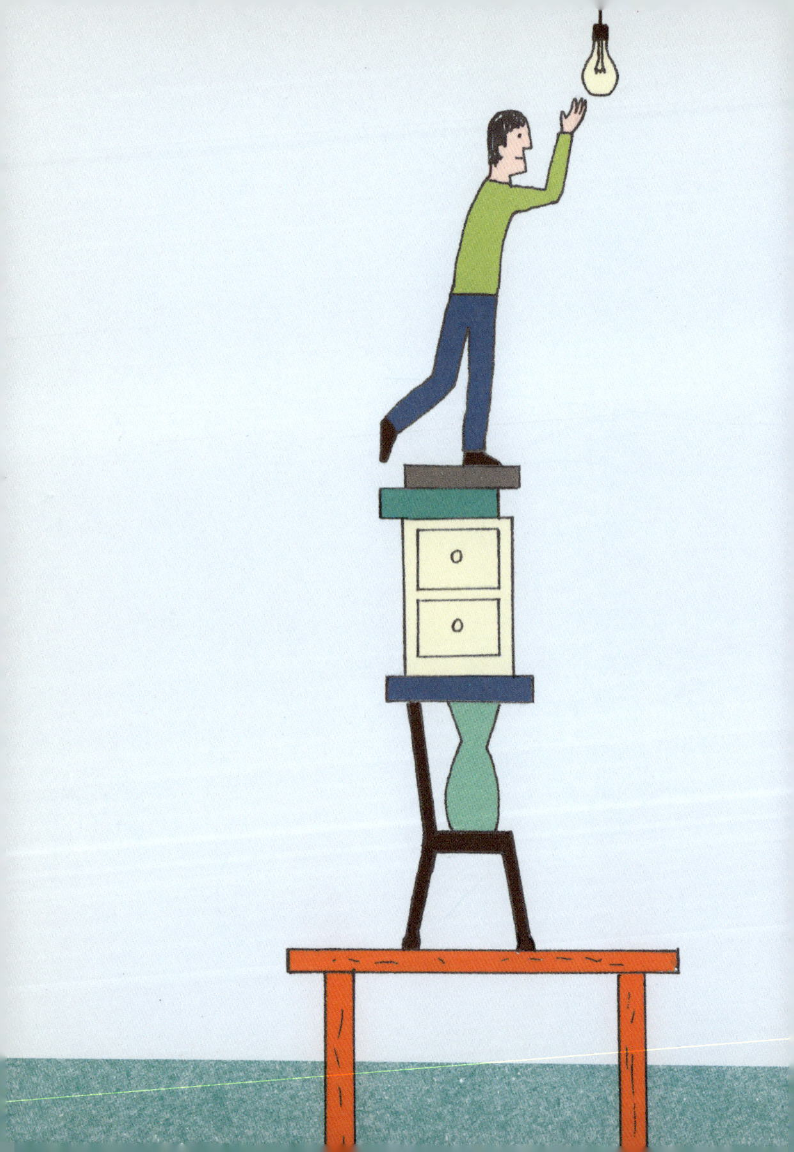

LIFE IS REALLY SIMPLE BUT WE INSIST ON MAKING IT COMPLICATED.

LIFE IS A PARTY.

Life is a gift.

LIFE IS SWEET.

Life is scary.

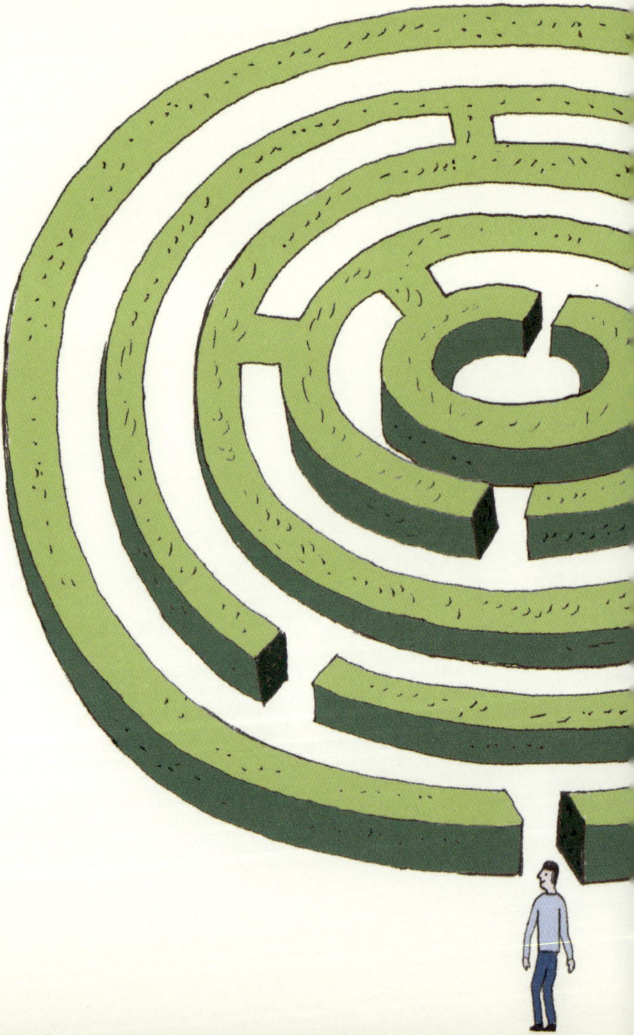

Life is a challenge—meet it.

Life is a song worth singing.

Life is a work of art.

Life is like a box of chocolates.
You never know what you're
gonna get.

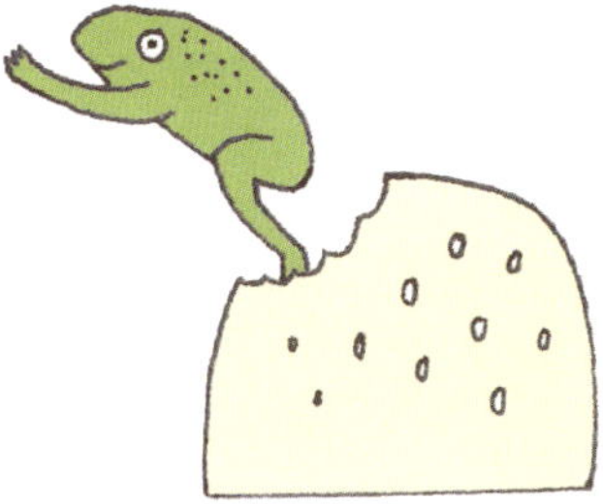

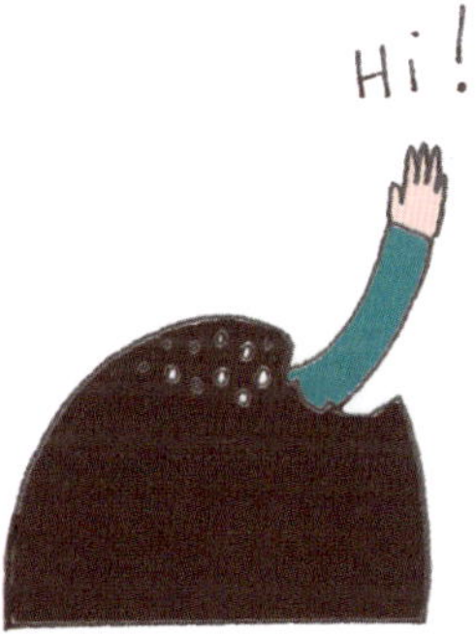
Hi!

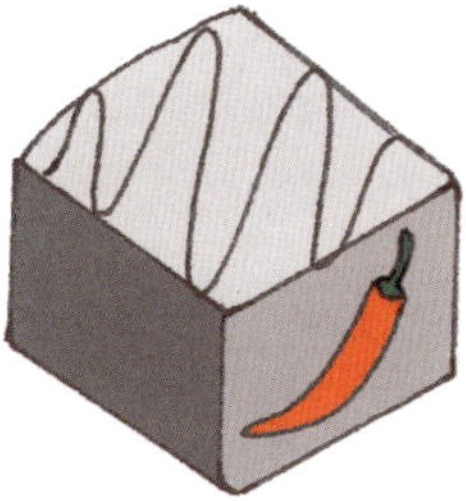

LIFE IS A SEXUALLY TRANSMITTED
TERMINAL DISEASE.

Life is better when you're laughing.

Life is like
riding a bicycle.

To keep your balance you must keep moving.

LIFE IS AN IMPROVISATION. YOU HAVE NO IDEA WHAT'S GOING TO HAPPEN NEXT AND YOU ARE MOSTLY JUST MAKING THINGS UP AS YOU GO ALONG.

Life is like a canvas: it starts out blank and every day is like another brush stroke.

LIFE IS
EITHER
A DARING
ADVENTURE
OR
NOTHING.

Life is a glorious cycle of song,
A medley of extemporanea;
And love is a thing that can never go wrong;
And I am Marie of Romania.

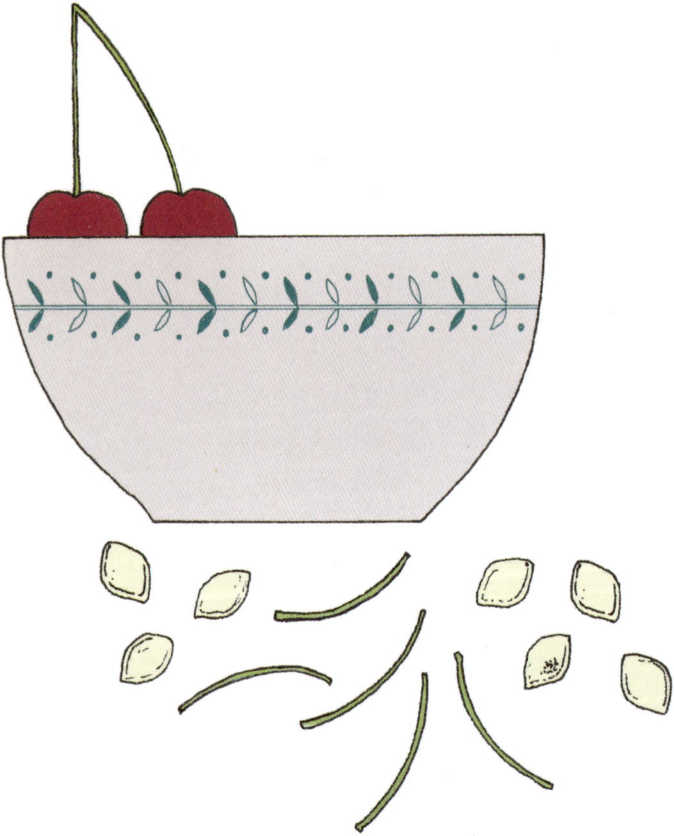

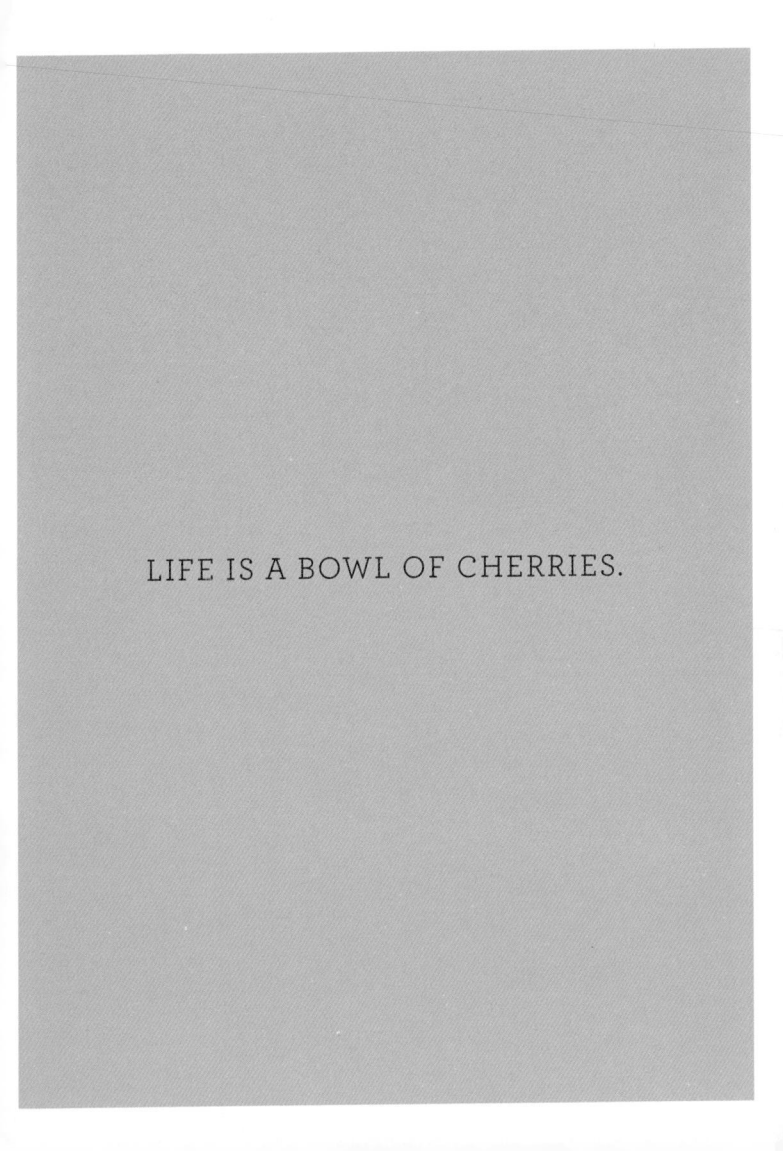

LIFE IS A BOWL OF CHERRIES.

LIFE IS A TEST.

LIFE IS TOUGH.

LIFE IS A RIVER.

Life is a highway.

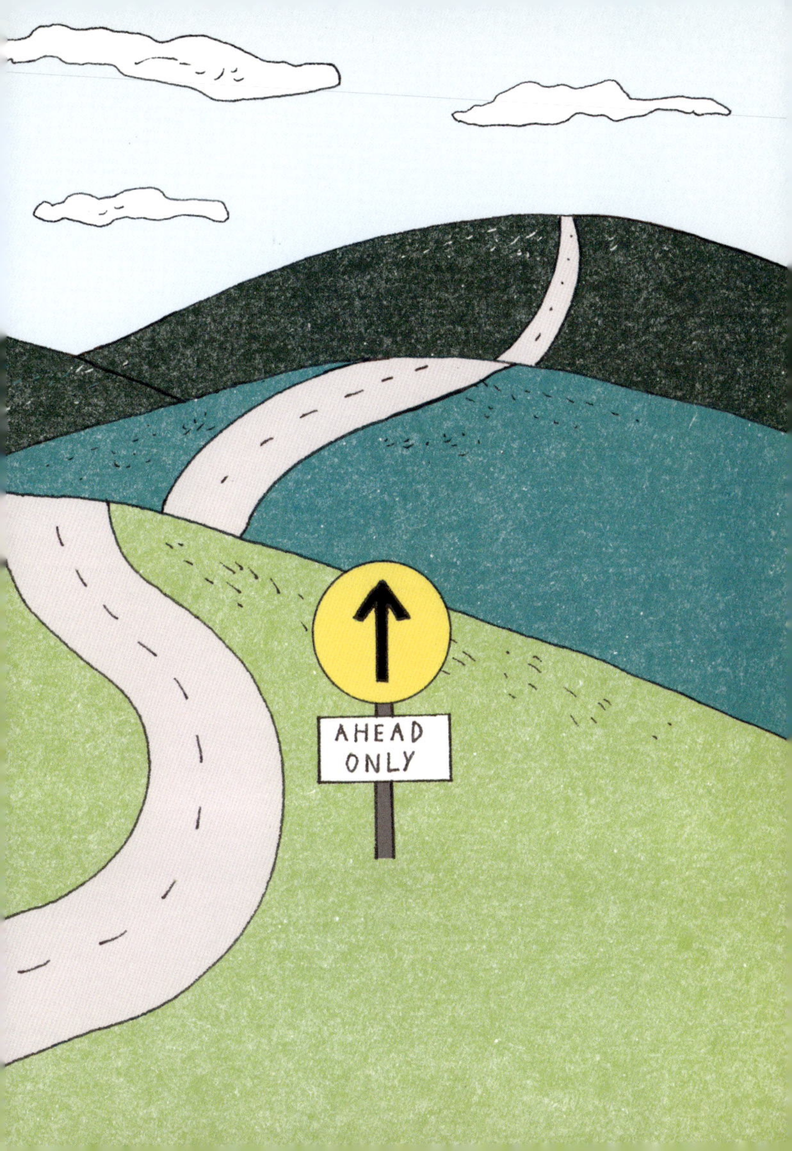
AHEAD
ONLY

Life is 10% what happens to you and 90% how you respond to it.

LIFE IS LIKE MATH—IF SOMETHING IS EASY, YOU'RE DOING IT WRONG.

LIFE IS ABOUT...

THE PEOPLE YOU MEET.

LIFE IS ABOUT CHANGE.

Life is a fairytale.

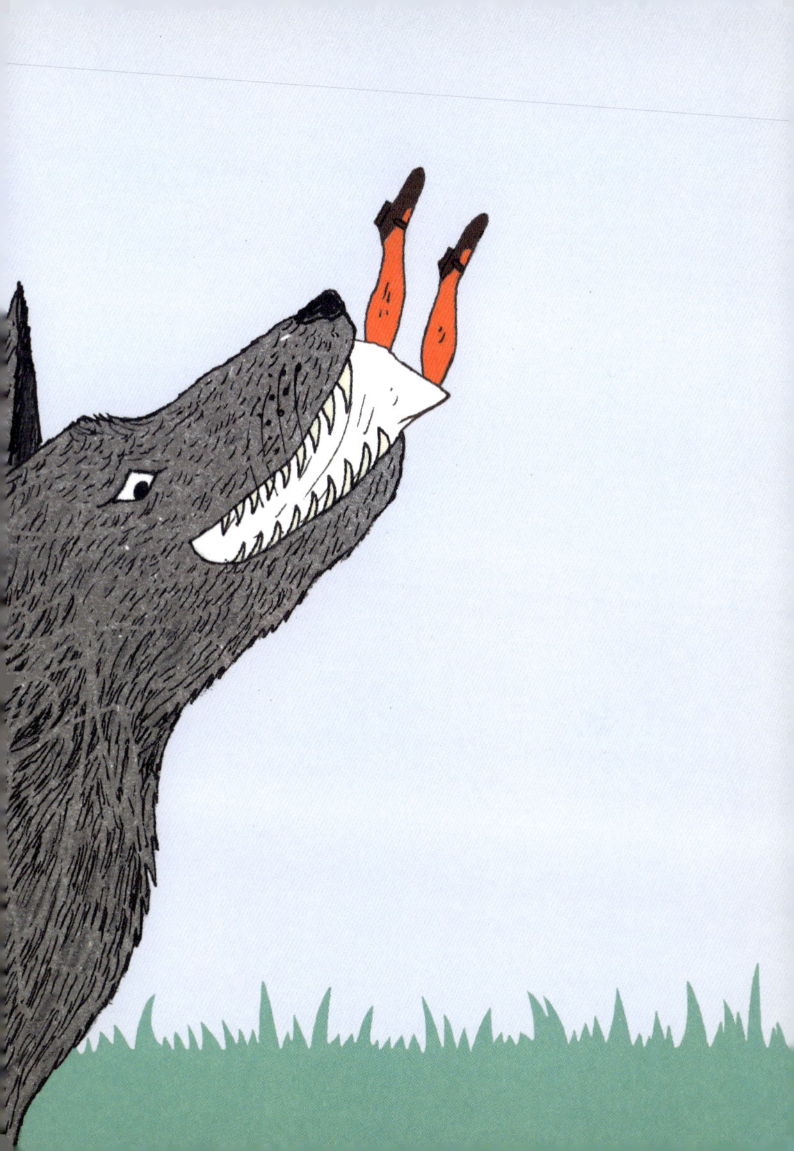

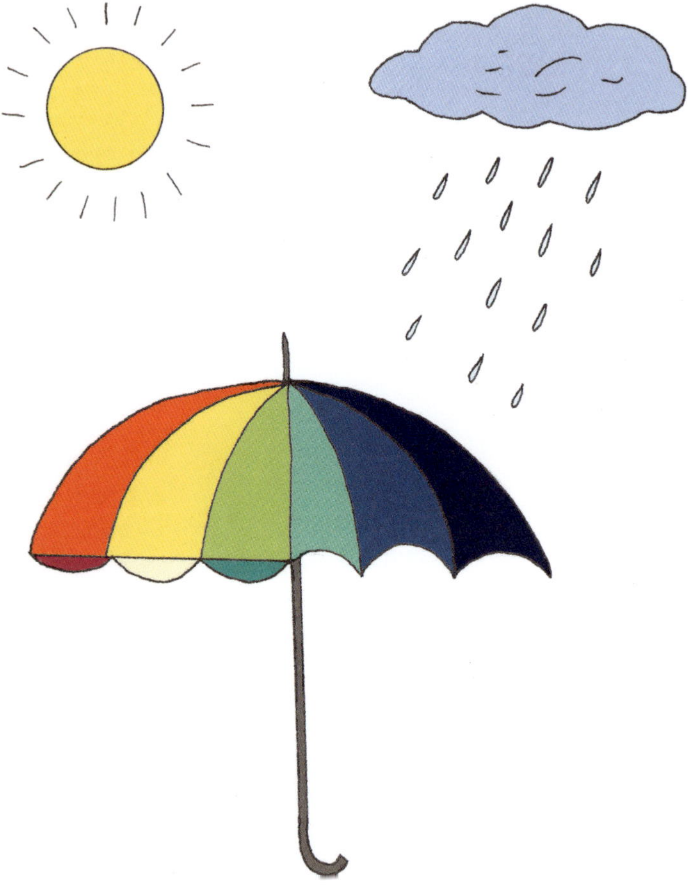

LIFE IS LIKE A RAINBOW: IT TAKES BOTH THE SUN AND THE RAIN TO MAKE THE COLORS APPEAR.

Life is made up of

marble

and mud.

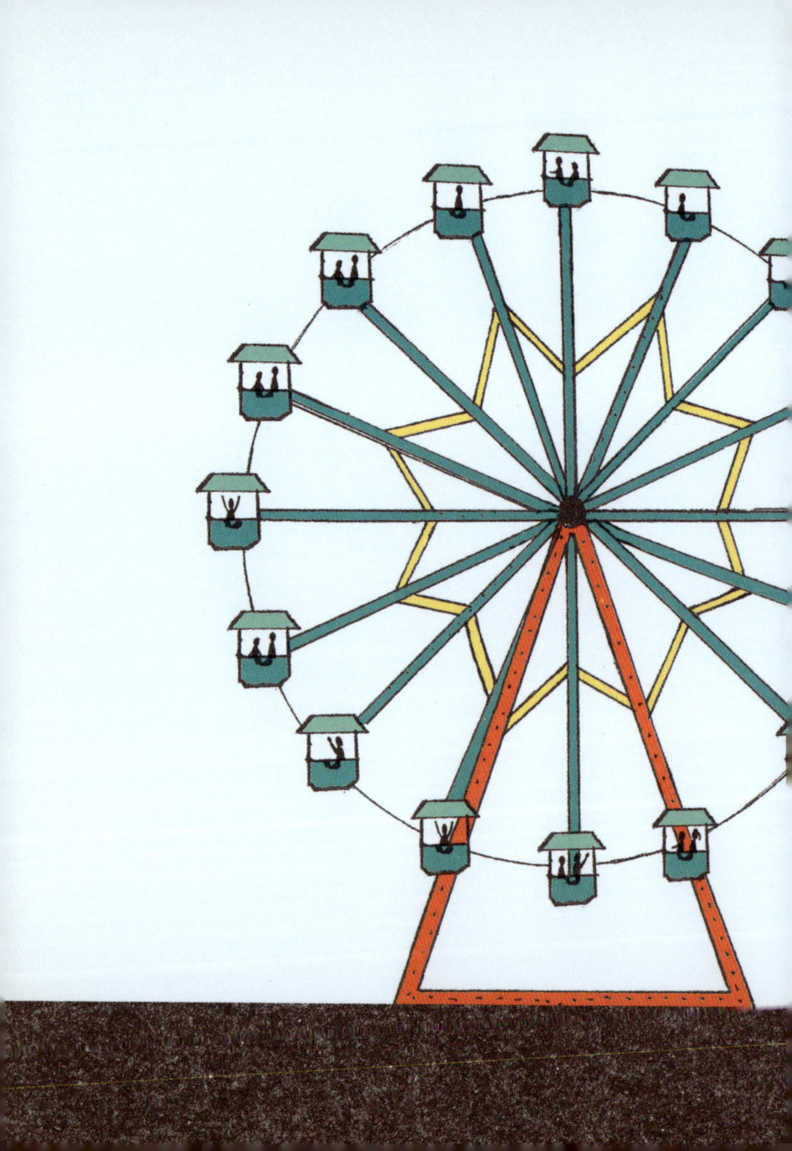

LIFE IS A CARNIVAL.

LIFE IS A TRAGEDY WHEN SEEN IN CLOSE-UP BUT A COMEDY IN LONG SHOT.

Life is a puzzle.

LIFE IS A ZOO IN

THE JUNGLE.

Life is better than
death, I believe,
if only because it
is less boring, and
because it has fresh
peaches in it.

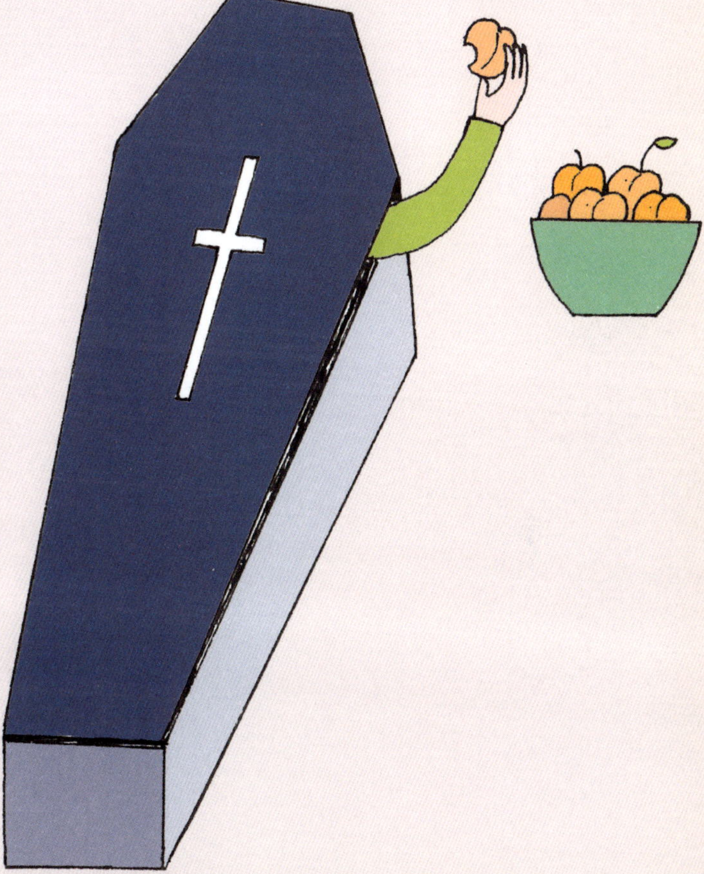

Life is beautiful.

LIFE IS RANDOM.

Life is a do-it-yourself project.

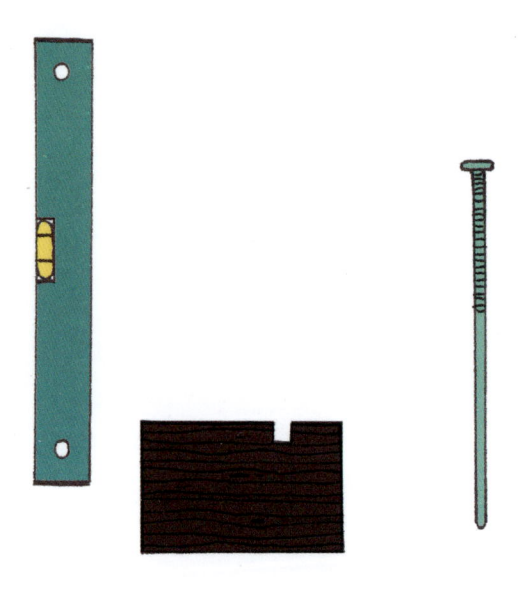

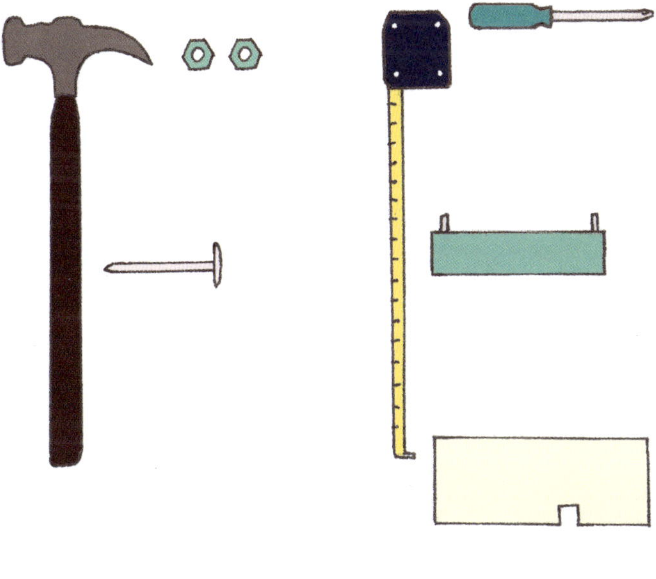

Life is a play, and we are all actors on a stage.

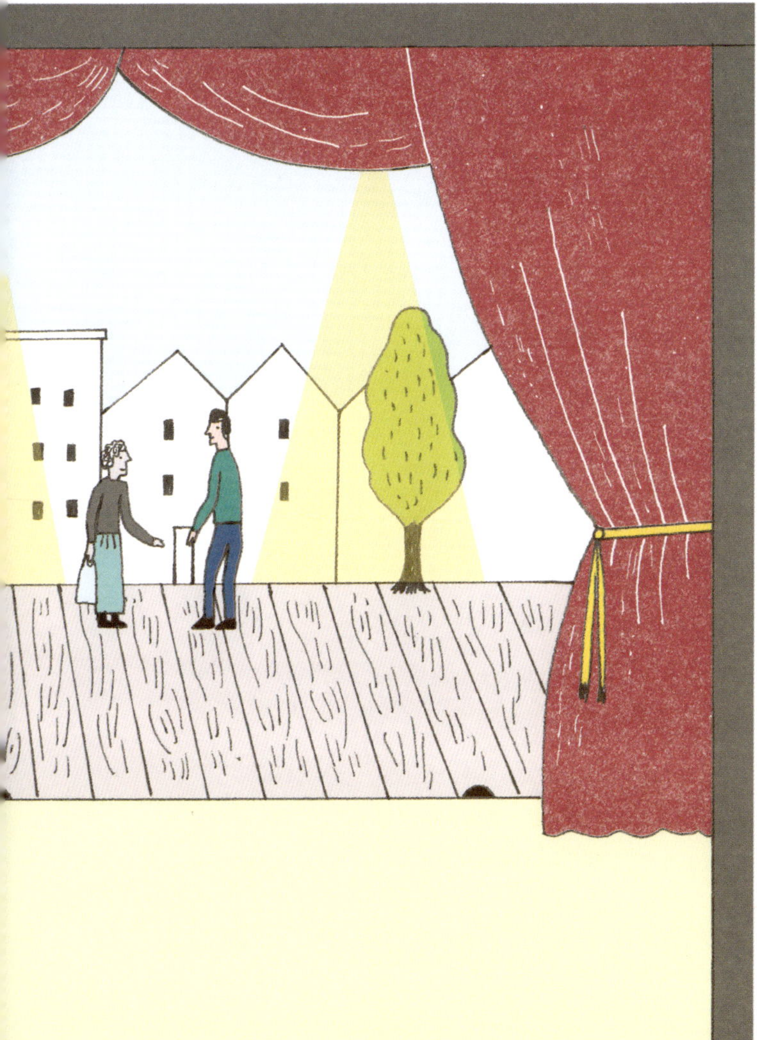

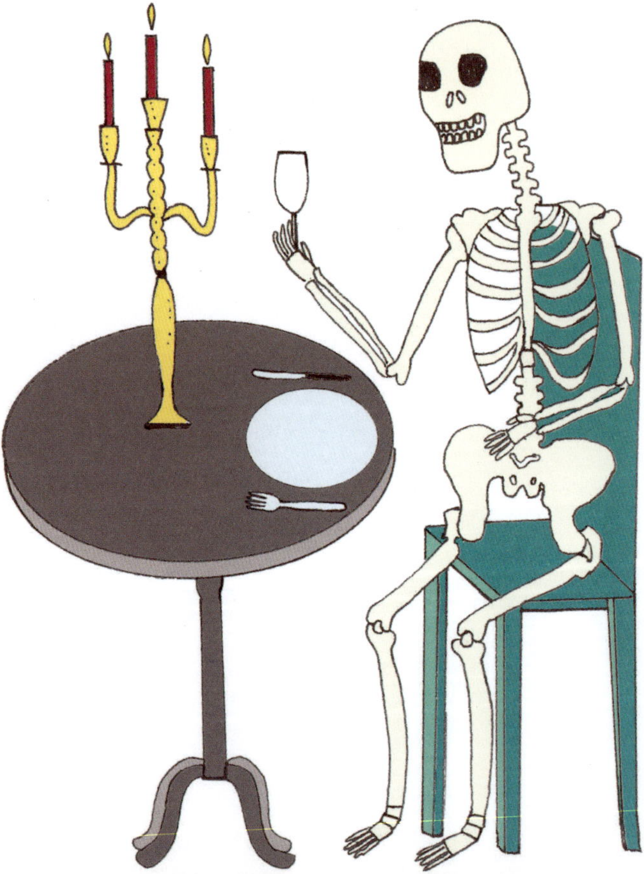

Life is
a banquet,
and some
poor suckers
are starving
to death.

Life is like a book: some chapters are happy, some are sad, but if you never turn the page you'll never know what the next chapter has in store for you.

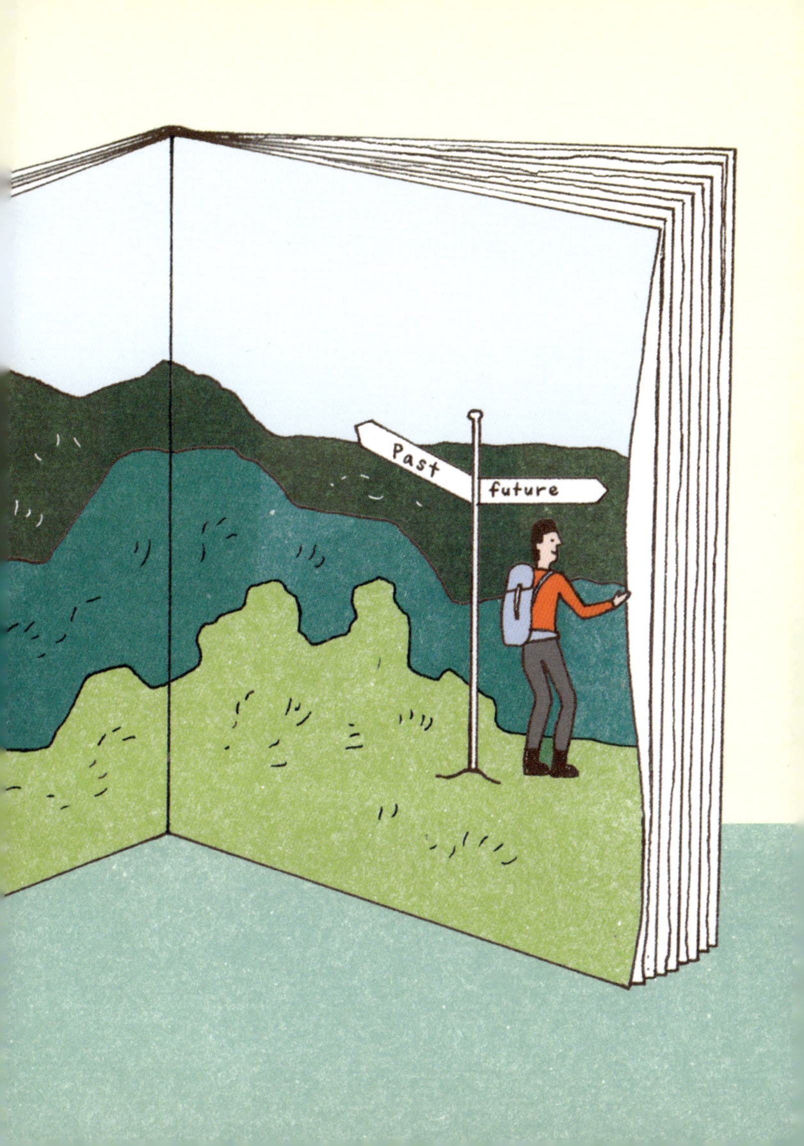
Past
future

ATTRIBUTIONS

"Life is what happens to you while you're busy making other plans." —JOHN LENNON

"Life is just one damn thing after another." —ELBERT HUBBARD

"Life is not having been told that the man has just waxed the floor." —OGDEN NASH

"Life is like a box of chocolates. You never know what you're gonna get." —FORREST GUMP

"Life is like riding a bicycle. To keep your balance you must keep moving." —ALBERT EINSTEIN

"Life is either a daring adventure or nothing." —HELEN KELLER

"Life is a glorious cycle of song, A medley of extemporanea; And love is a thing that can never go wrong; And I am Marie of Romania." —DOROTHY PARKER

"Life is a highway." —RASCAL FLATTS

"Life is made up of marble and mud."
—NATHANIEL HAWTHORNE

"Life is a tragedy when seen in close-up but a comedy in long shot." —CHARLIE CHAPLIN

"Life is a zoo in the jungle." —PETER DE VRIES

"Life is better than death, I believe, if only because it is less boring, and because it has fresh peaches in it."
—ALICE WALKER

"Life is a banquet, and some poor suckers are starving to death." —PATRICK DENNIS

Life is a metaphor.